The Path to Hope

Stéphane Hessel
Edgar Morin

Translated from the French by Antony Shugaar
With a foreword by Jeff Madrick

OTHER PRESS NEW YORK

Case design by Andreas Gurewich
Production Editor: Yvonne E. Cárdenas
Book design: Cassandra J. Pappas
This book was typeset in 11pt Dante by Alpha Design &
Composition of Pittsfield, NH

10 9 8 7 6 5 4 3 2 1

Library of Congress Cataloging-in-Publication Data

Hessel, Stéphane.
  [Chemin de l'espérance. English]
  The path to hope / by Stéphane Hessel and Edgar Morin
; translated from the French by Antony Shugaar ; with a
foreword by Jeff Madrick.
    p. cm.
  ISBN 978-1-59051-560-0 (hardcover) — ISBN 978-1-59051-
561-7 (e-book)
  1. Social policy.   2. Economic policy.   3. Equality.
4. Quality of life.   5. World politics—21st century.
I. Morin, Edgar.   II. Shugaar, Antony.   III. Title.
  HN18.3.H4713 2012
  306—dc23

                                    2011053134

Contents

The Road to Hope

Jeff Madrick

Look at the facts on the ground, say Stéphane Hessel and Edgar Morin, if not precisely in those words. Don't tell us about theory. Economic theory has led us to social failure. Simply look around you.

These ninety-somethings are outraged. Hessel worked in the French Resistance during World War II and was shaped by its ultimate victory over French Vichyism and the creation in the late 1950s of what he believes was a true French Republic successfully dedicated to equality. His book *Time for Outrage* called on people around the world to "resist" again. This recent short book sold over a million copies in France and inspired protest everywhere.

Now, in *The Path to Hope*, only slightly longer, Hessel and his friend and peer, the eminent sociologist Edgar Morin, tell us what to protest against—the strangling economic power of finance and the shocking spread of ethnic prejudice among nations that were once proud carriers of humanism and the resulting loss of community and what they call fellow feeling.

It is purist free-market economics and its rising power that both men despise. Their rhetoric is not mild. To them, finance capitalism could become the new fascism. It is already some way down that road, suppressing the citizens of both rich and poor nations. This is what they witnessed during the rise of Vichy France, they argue: a plutocracy frightened of bolshevism that might jeopardize their fortunes turned too easily to fascism.

The spread of a purist ethnic movement in Europe is the other enemy of their humanist ideals. Hessel was a contributor to the beautiful language of the United Nations' Universal Declaration of Human Rights, adopted in 1948 under the guidance of Eleanor Roosevelt. Here is a relevant passage: "Everyone, as a member of society, has the right to social security and is entitled to realization, through national effort and international co-operation . . . , of the economic, social and cultural rights indispensable for his dignity and the free development of his personality." This ideal, he and Morin believe, is now being betrayed.

One doesn't have to agree with everything they write to be moved by them and to understand that in fundamental ways they are right. Their true enemy is not economic inequality or even the persistence of poverty but *injustice* itself. And so it is with Occupy Wall Street. So it is with the brave protesters of the Arab Spring, the *indignados* of Spain, the occupiers of St. Paul's, the Israelis angry with their government's policies. They all say the same thing.

In brutal dictatorships, the protesters want a voice, they want a basic democracy. In rich

.nocracies, however, the protesters also want a voice lost to the power of money. They want a true democracy as well.

Free us of a tyranny, say the Egyptians and the Libyans. Don't feed us the stories of the benefits of a free-market economy, say the protesters in rich nations. It hasn't worked. (And make no mistake, the protesters of the Arab Spring link their tyrannical former regimes with the power of money in the West.) The economics of self-interest and minimal government has led us down a path of self-destruction, say Hessel and Morin, and many others. You ask us how to reform your economic systems and we answer that you should tell us why you still believe in them.

Simply look around and you find injustice almost everywhere. Poverty envelops the world, still. Hessel and Morin simplify here. Formally, poverty by some measures has fallen. But the definition of poverty according to the World Bank is tragicomically low. And the gap between rich and poor has grown enormously.

Meanwhile, income inequality has risen in virtually every rich nation since 1980. The share of wages in GDP has also fallen significantly in most rich nations over the same period, even in China. In the rich nations, public transportation is widely neglected, teachers are increasingly devalued, pollution abounds, and the climate is radically changing. Anti-immigrant movements are flourishing and gaining respectability almost everywhere we look, partly as a result of the poor performance of economies. America's private prisons make lots of money by locking up so-called illegal immigrants. America has proportionally more people in prison—not only illegal immigrants, of course—than any other rich nation. Private prisons are a major new industry.

Hessel and Morin have written this book to present a plan for action, not merely to make known their outrage and stimulate the outrage of others. Their plan is, to say the least, broad, too abstract. It is their path to hope not to ultimate solutions. They want to reinvigorate the values of Europe's humanism. Few see Europe as the world's leader, but the values of the Enlightenment and European humanism can be a guide. They are essentially true, and they have been a source of American ideals since the Colonial era. Hessel and Morin's proposals are useful less as a blueprint than as a call for attention to injustice and failure. Basically, they want "fellow feeling" to return. They want community to reign again. They want education to be revamped to teach the young how to live fuller, less materialistic lives. They quote Rousseau: "Life is the trade I want to teach him." They want the adolescent rebels of France and elsewhere to be saved. They want bureaucracies to be revitalized.

What breaks their hearts most is the loss of compassion. Without bonds and traditions, cultures of decency, and everyday evidence of the caring of others, they wonder how civilization will survive. Finance capitalism has not provided that. To the contrary, the race for self-aggrandizement undermines the possibilities.

They would like centers in every community that are "sources of friendship and care for others." They want citizens to participate in civil services to deal collectively with natural disasters.

If their ideas are impractical, so be it. Take them as they are, they seem to say. They march on through this book. And they can be poignant. Adolescence to them is magical, for example, the time in which so much must be formed, a time when all is so malleable and can easily go so wrong.

Frankly, they sometimes sound like bad ads. They want to "globalize and deglobalize." They speak of "humanizing the cities and revitalizing the countryside."

But there is a kernel of truth, often a large one, in all the propositions. "The path toward a politics based on the quality of life cannot be undertaken and developed unless we make up our minds to throttle the octopus of finance capitalism and the barbarity of national purification and ethnic cleansing," they write. In France, they want a "permanent council to fight inequality," another permanent council to reverse the fall in the proportion of GDP that goes to wages, another to protect the environment. They would impose tariffs on nations that make goods on the backs of abused workers or forbid unionization. They would reduce financial speculation. They would revive education to make it not a linear recitation of cause and effect but a circular understanding of how the world works, each event feeding another with constant feedback. No summa of truths but a dialectic, they say.

It is impossible not to notice their idealism. They offer not so much plans for concrete action as a set of broad and mostly necessary principles. The Occupy Wall Streeters are subject to a similar criticism. If you are serious, we ask them, what are your specific, practical demands?

Some of the American protesters are trying to devise workable plans to change bits of America. But perhaps the wiser of them are, more importantly, trying to shine the American light on injustice and bring voice to the disenfranchised, the unlistened to, the confused, and the angry. We have heard all the solutions, they seem to be saying. But we want to be sure someone is listening.

There is no voice without listeners, no sounds in the forest when the tree falls if no one is there. Washington has not listened, the occupiers are generally saying, so we need another path besides traditional government to get them to listen, and to get others to listen. The media mostly reflect the narrow, conventional conversations in Washington.

To these people, Hessel and Morin are especially relevant. Occupy Wall Street also says look around us. Do we want to make some small quick fixes to our economy, or do we want to talk more broadly of a deeper trouble? Many of them are choosing the latter. This mystifies people like Mayor Mike Bloomberg of New York City, who made his vast fortune on Wall Street. Men and women like Bloomberg can't help but believe Wall Street is a great job creator and that these protesters should go get a job, start a business, as if opportunity is simply there for those who grab it, as if the American dream is as alive as it ever was, as if the unemployment rate for those in their twenties hasn't soared to 15 to 20 percent.

In one speech after he evicted Occupy Wall Street from Zuccotti Park, Bloomberg said the protesters will now have to live by the power of their ideas. Implicitly, he was saying, if you want a financial transactions tax or a tax on the wealthy or a new mortgage relief program, go fight for it.

But imagine how the protesters feel about this man, who apparently thinks he became mayor on the power of his ideas. Bloomberg spent more than $250 million of his own money on three mayoral campaigns. There lay the power of his ideas. It is but one of many examples of a disconnection of values and down-on-the-ground experience between those at the top of the income spectrum and everyone else. To say that these men and women at the top are out of touch is an understatement.

What of the science of economics? The main arrogance of contemporary mainstream economics is that free-market policies are increasingly proposed as a path not only to prosperity but also to social justice. This was the revolution of Milton Friedman, who wrote just this in his popular book *Capitalism and Freedom* (1962), and was carried forward to a lesser but still potent degree by former Keynesians like Lawrence Summers, the former U.S. treasury secretary, who proudly talked as late as 2001 about how he favored market solutions in many areas over government solutions. In the process, Summers condoned Alan Greenspan's Ayn Rand–influenced free-market ideology toward financial regulation. To take one example, with the advice of Summers and former treasury secretary Robert Rubin, Bill Clinton used the tax increase he passed in 1993, and the budget surpluses being generated, to pay down debt so that private markets could allocate more money, so that the market could work to improve welfare. He invested far less in infrastructure or education, his priority fueling the private markets.

Economics can be powerful and constructive. But free-market economics, the prevailing view, has not led to social justice, and cannot on its own. Belief in such propositions enabled the Wall Street crisis, as unfettered finance capitalism led to speculative bubbles and misdirected capital. Government stepped back under Clinton and Bush and Greenspan. In many respects, it has become the era of economic theory, the narrow but widely advocated version of which served the plutocracy well. Summers, Greenspan, and Rubin refused to allow derivatives, those low-down-payment securities based on other securities that were the heart of the financial crisis, to be regulated. They were essentially traded in secret with no government demands for capital to back up the promises of traders. Free-market competition would weed out the trustworthy from the untrustworthy, Summers and his allies in the Clinton administration argued. Bankers made vast personal fortunes.

Consider what has happened as the Friedman-Summers model ascended. Wages have generally stagnated for most workers as corporate profits have soared. Inequality is breathtakingly high. Poverty rates are as high as they were in the mid-1960s before the war on poverty was fully implemented. The quality of education and the

adequacy of infrastructure are frightfully dete-
riorated. Unemployment rates will not return to
acceptable levels for many years. Some twenty-
five million Americans cannot find a full-time
job. Some twenty million full-time workers earn
poverty wages. A higher proportion of Americans earn less than two-thirds of the median income than in any other rich nation.

The young, in particular, have high unemployment levels and low starting salaries, and
are saddled with enormous debt taken on to pay
unjustifiably expensive university tuitions. And
in terms of cost, and increasingly in terms of
delivery of services, health care in America is a
tragedy whose most painful future consequences
remain mostly neglected, even if Obama's health
program is not reversed.

Small wonder that a right-wing populist movement like the Tea Party takes hold. Small wonder that anti-immigrant policies are so much a
part of Republican presidential campaigns. Small
wonder that some are trying to restrict the voting
of those they disagree with.

I imagine two circles. One is the circle of free-market economics, the Friedman circle, in which both prosperity and social justice are optimized. The other is the circle of community, government, and fellow feeling, of social programs, fair taxes, and a commitment to equality. This is the Hessel-Morin circle.

The Friedman circle grew bigger in the last forty years, the Hessel-Morin circle smaller, especially in America. Friedman believed that self-reliance and competition would produce more secure retirement, better jobs, and lower unemployment if the other circle did not get in the way.

In the twentieth century, America worked best when these circles were roughly the same size, and when they overlapped. Perhaps the Hessel-Morin circle should be larger than the Friedman circle. But each circle should tolerate the other, work with the other—as I say, overlap.

I am not sure that Hessel and Morin want the circles to overlap. They leave some room for capitalism—perhaps not enough room. Equality is a beautiful idea, as is universal human rights. These rights, however, should also include the right of a man and woman to start a business, to wake up one morning with a new idea for a product and pursue it with vigor and optimism. This, too, is beautiful. I doubt Hessel and Morin would disagree. But that power has gone too far the wrong way. Hessel and Morin have seen too much destruction of their values. They have been around. They have seen undiluted, cruel fascism and faced it down. They see the potential for it to rise again. They want large-scale change. So, I think, do many of America's occupiers. Hessel and Morin call for "a broad insurrection of conscience." That is a lovely description of Occupy Wall Street, as well. But, maybe most important, they are concerned with life. They want a new politics "based on a yearning to live and restore life." For this, they need a return of community, not the atomization of unregulated capitalism. I'd say, again, an overlapping of the circles. Even some economists are beginning to think in such broader terms. Alas, not enough of them.

The Path to Hope

One

Our Country and Its Place in the World

Dear fellow citizens,

It is our intent to denounce in this book the blindly wrongheaded course that has been set by our politicians, as well as the policies that will ultimately lead us to disaster.

It is our intent to chart a political path to national salvation.

It is our intent to declare a new hope.

Our Nation, the World, and Europe

Our nation does not exist in a vacuum; we do not live in a static world.

We must understand that our planet's fate is in our hands. We are now all vulnerable to the mortal threats posed by the proliferation of nuclear weapons, the spread of ethnic and religious conflicts, the degradation of our environment, the dubious progress brought to us by a completely uncontrolled world economy, the tyranny of money, and the convergence of two forms of barbarity: one that is as old as history itself, and a more recent one, the barbarity of technological and economic opportunism.

After humanity survived the horrors of the twentieth century's various forms of totalitarianism, the threat of finance capitalism now rears its ugly head. At the same time, a bewildering array of ethnic, nationalistic, and religious fanaticism and extremism is loosed upon the world. In fact, a convergence of crises constitutes the greatest single danger that humanity has ever faced. In essence, the impending menace is this: Humanity is unable to attain humanity.

In 1932, Paul Valéry wrote with a lucidity that could not be any more timely: "Never before has mankind combined so much power with so much confusion, so many fears and so many playthings, so much knowledge and so much uncertainty. Disquiet and futility share out our days."[1]

Some years later, Konrad Lorenz wrote: "We must ask ourselves what does more damage to the mind of modern man: his blinding greed for money or his enervating haste."[2] And the answer is both: one linked to the other, one reinforcing the other. Or, as Wordsworth would say, "Getting and spending, we lay waste our powers."

We have a duty as citizens of the planet—citizens with a stake in the fate of all people on Earth—to subscribe to certain universal principles. Those principles were first expressed in the platform adopted in 1944 by the National Council of the French Resistance; they were further refined four years later in the Universal Declaration of Human Rights.

We cannot ourselves determine the fate of our planet. We can, however, chart a long, daunting, momentous path that leads to the creation of a single Homeland Earth. Such a worldwide homeland could encompass as well as safeguard the individual homelands, and it would do so in the name of the principles set forth in those texts. This means we have to abolish the absolute sovereignty of all nation-states in order to take on the challenges of the planetwide problems of the global era, but we would be able to preserve that sovereignty in all other sectors.

Even as free-market capitalism claims to replace all other ideologies, it has shown itself to be a failed ideology. Its laissez-faire policies might have achieved some partial success, but overall it impoverished far more people than it ever enriched. Under its aegis, globalization, development, and westernization—three aspects of a single phenomenon—all proved incapable of solving the vital problems of mankind.

The fact that the global system is helpless to solve the fundamental problems that it creates ultimately condemns it to a fate of disintegration or regression. The one alternative path is for that system to create the conditions for its own metamorphosis; only by transforming itself can it hope to survive.

Our global system is thus condemned to choose between death and transformation. This transformation can take place only as the outcome of a variety of processes of reform and change, each of them a tributary to a single mighty river of metamorphosis. In this way, our era of change is a prelude to a greater, epochal change.

We must understand that globalization constitutes both the best and the worst thing that could ever happen to mankind.

The best because all the scattered fragments of humanity have become interdependent for the first time, creating a shared fate that makes one single Homeland Earth possible. Such an outcome, far from eliminating individual homelands, would simply incorporate them.

The worst because it has triggered a frantic race toward a succession of catastrophes.

The uncontrolled rise of the destructive, manipulative powers of science and technology and the unleashing in all directions of profit-driven economics have led to the proliferation of weapons of mass destruction and the deterioration of the environment. At the same time, the various forms of twentieth-century totalitarianism have been replaced by a form of finance capitalism entirely without borders. This finance capitalism subjugates nations and peoples to its unbridled speculation. Alongside it, we see the return and growth of closed-minded xenophobia and racial, ethnic, and territorial prejudice and hostility. The combined ravages of financial speculation and blind fanaticism and extremism have only amplified and accelerated the processes that herald impending catastrophes.

We must therefore be aware that even as the process of development now under way does dispense Western-style prosperity to a small fraction of the world's population, it has also produced vast areas of poverty and fostered gigantic levels of inequality.

It is crucial that we both globalize and deglobalize. We must pursue and encourage the kinds
of globalization that foster a shared future for
human beings from all walks of life and everywhere on Earth—a future that will protect us
from a grim array of mortal dangers. We must
all band together in solidarity to safeguard this
planet whose existence is so crucial to our own
well-being. It is in our own urgent interest to save
Mother Earth. We advocate encouraging and developing every aspect of globalization that fosters
fellowship and cultural vitality. Simultaneously,
however, we propose restoring full independence
of action at the local, regional, and national levels, thus safeguarding and encouraging cultural
diversity everywhere. We must deglobalize in
order to offer full scope to the economics of social solidarity, safeguard the economic viability of
local agriculture, and preserve small-scale farming as well as craftsmanship and local trade. Only
by so doing can we hope to reverse the desolation

and abandonment of the countryside and the critical reduction of services available to withering and moribund outlying areas, such as rural districts and periurban slums.

It is important to recognize that the standard formula for development completely ignores the ties of fellowship and the power of working together. That formula also ignores the lore and practical knowledge of traditional societies. We must rethink and diversify modern development to ensure that it preserves the invaluable forms of fellowship that are integral to the community ethos.

In parallel, starting at home, we must replace the single-minded imperative of growth with a more complex and nuanced imperative that distinguishes between what we need to increase and what we need to diminish. We ought to encourage the growth of green energy, public transportation, and a socially responsible form of economics that involves solidarity and fellowship. We should likewise focus on schools, culture, and urban planning and development designed to humanize the world's big cities. We also need to reduce our dependence on industrialized agriculture, fossil-based energy sources, and nuclear power. We must fight the parasitic role of middlemen, weapons industries that profit from war, endemic consumer addiction, the economics of the superfluous and the superficial, and our deep-rooted spendthrift lifestyle based on getting and squandering. The time has come to draw up a single list of the things that should grow and the things that should be reduced.

In an increasingly multipolar world, it is crucial that we strengthen and unify the Western democracies in an effort to address the largest and most urgent problems standing in the way of peace and human understanding. Europe, for instance, should immediately develop a coordinated policy for the integration of immigrants into civil society. Europe also needs to take a leadership role in defusing the radicalization and conflicts that are the cause of so much barbarity in our world. Those conflicts must be addressed, wherever they are unleashed, wherever they fester. A case in point is the ongoing Israeli-Palestinian tragedy. This clash has metastasized into a planet-spanning cancer.

We envision a crucial role for the Western world and Europe in particular. Just as the European Renaissance of the fifteenth and sixteenth centuries engendered a new blossoming of civilization by incorporating ancient Greek and Roman thought, we urge striving to bring about a latter-day Renaissance by adopting the moral and spiritual contributions of other cultures. In particular, we advise looking to Asian wisdom. We need to offer the world something more than a mere perpetuation of westernization. Let us offer, instead, a political approach based on humanism. Such an approach respects the distinctive features and the resources of various cultures, and also takes into account their peculiarities and shortcomings. It strives to create a synthesis of the best of all civilizations. The idea of such a symbiosis among civilizations ought to dispel once and for all the idea of culture shock or a war of civilizations.

Within the context of Western society, we should continue developing humanistic forms of behavior, an effective system of democracy, and respect for the rights of men and women everywhere.

At the same time, while recognizing that the great metamorphosis can take place only in the context of a complex and multiform process, we propose—here and now—that the nations of Earth adopt a form of worldwide governance that not only reforms and refounds the United Nations on a new basis but also creates global contexts for decision making in the face of such vital challenges as the proliferation of weapons of mass destruction, the deterioration of the biosphere, the resurgence of famine, and the persistence of malnutrition. Such world governance requires the full-scale implementation of economic regulation. By so doing, we would restrict and curtail the misdeeds of worldwide financial speculators, including the gouging and profiteering inherent in the manipulation of prices for raw materials.

In many cases around the world, our society's race to the bottom has triggered explosive situations. Anger prompted by rising inequality has provided justification and focus for the proliferation of indigenous uprisings everywhere.

The insolent cynicism of the corrupt and endemic levels of unemployment are just a few of the traits common to the revolts of the Arab Spring, the unrest of the indigenous peoples of Spain, Greece, Israel, and Chile, the rioters in London and other major British cities, and the Indian uprisings.

We are well aware of how critical and delicate a moment this is for humanity. We see the ambiguity of this juncture; we perceive the risks and perils. We also see the enormous opportunities.

Two

Policies for Our Country

Under good government, poverty is shameful;
under bad government, wealth is shameful.
—CONFUCIUS

The true life is absent.
—ARTHUR RIMBAUD

There are many who believe that the increased
integration required by globalization tends to
undermine any independent national policies designed to challenge the constraints and evils that
spring from that very process of globalization.
If such policies were implemented, they say, it
would be impossible to benefit from the positive
aspects of globalization. We disagree: In the face

of this new challenge, a new political approach is possible. Such a policy would also blaze a path toward a radical regeneration of our society.

There are lots of people who clearly recognize just how dependent on globalization we are. Many of them feel a growing sense of helplessness. Overtaken by that sense of hopelessness and resignation, they plunge into a dark fatalism, turn away from politics, or are swept up in a wave of rage. Others react to the evils generated by our society's dependence on the rest of the world by withdrawing inward. They remain blind to the obvious truth that isolation and a closed society are a far greater evil than the ills they think they're escaping.

A new and independent national policy is possible. This political approach would follow the twofold principles we have set forth: globalize and deglobalize, develop and envelop. Deglobalization and envelopment, as we have pointed out, safeguard the vital interests of homelands and regions, while at the same time protecting living cultures. This twofold principle is the basis for a political approach that guarantees links of global and national solidarity, fellowship among the various local collectives, and the benefits of local farming. It would make possible the adoption of a deeply reformist and transformational political program within the context of a single national government.

Why Reform and Transform?

Let us begin by listing a series of negative factors: the unbridled lust for profits; the deterioration of solid bonds of fellow feeling; the hyperbureaucratization of both public and private administration; the intensity of cutthroat competition as fair trade degenerates under market pressures; the dominance of quantity over quality; the toxic nature of consumer culture that drives us to purchase products that possess illusory benefits at best; the sharp decline in the quality of food produced by industrialized agriculture and stockbreeding; the helplessness of consumers and small- and medium-scale manufacturers; a citizenry that is increasingly brainwashed and fragmented. Most important of all, the dire shortcomings of an educational system that fences off bodies of knowledge in such a way that it becomes impossible to deal with the fundamental and global challenges of our lives as individuals and as citizens in any organic manner. Finally, the looming crisis of a blind form of political thought that, in thrall to a generalized economic idiocy that subordinates all political problems to market issues, remains incapable of formulating any grand and overarching design.

Let us now recite the ills of our civilization: Where it has taken root, material prosperity has failed to bring about any real increase in happiness or mental well-being, as is evidenced by the unbridled consumption of illegal narcotics, anti-anxiety drugs, antidepressants, and sleeping pills by the well-to-do. The larger goal of societal well-being has been downgraded and restricted to personal material comforts. Economic development has not resulted in corresponding moral or ethical progress. The application of unrealistic deadlines, hyperspecialization, and compartmentalization to the workplace, the business world, political administrations, and ultimately to our very lives, has far too often resulted in spreading bureaucratization, the loss of initiative, and the avoidance of personal responsibility. The glittering success of individualism has brought with it the miserable deterioration of fellowship.

In our society there is a shortage of empathy, sympathy, and compassion. It takes the form of indifference and a lack of courtesy, often between neighbors and residents in the same apartment building. To say hello or good morning when you meet a stranger acknowledges that person as a human being who is deserving of fellow feeling. By the same token, there is often an estrangement among members of a single company, or even a single family. When a shared sense of mission is replaced by mere personal professional ambition, the previous love in the care given by physicians and hospitals is lost. The same thing happens in teaching, because, to use Plato's words, "You must have eros in order to teach," that is to say, love for both what you are teaching and those you are teaching. As the philosopher Axel Honneth rightly points out, "It is only through the experience of love that anyone can attain self-confidence." The supreme form of the recognition of others is love.

Hence the malaise within the larger context of well-being, the loneliness of millions of individuals in our midst, the increasing number of calls to suicide hotlines. Hence the wide array of consequences: alcoholism, drug abuse, depression, psychic maladies that are symptoms of the loosening of the ties of social reliance (social and family solidarity, and the like). Let us add to this list the myriad minor ills that overwhelm, disrupt, and blight our lives: the endless lines at ticket windows, in banks, in emergency rooms; being sent from one office to another, from one window to the next, the result of overworked employees, in turn a product of overspecialization, each sealed into his or her small domain of expertise, or else the reduction of staff in the name of efficiency and competition. It is not only consumers and people seeking public services who suffer from the overwork and specialization of employees. Those employees themselves suffer from on-the-job stress, psychosomatic illness, depression, even suicide. We must smash the rising tide of bureaucracy and suppress excessive competition.

At the same time, the finest achievements of our own history are coming under fire. The French example is striking: Over the course of the twentieth century, secular, social, republican France had driven into the background a rival France—which was reactionary, closed-minded, xenophobic, racist, and authoritarian. It took World War II, the greatest military disaster that our country has ever suffered, before this second France—waxing nostalgic for authoritarian and reactionary ideas of the past, the xenophobic and racist France that is hostile to all that is foreign, the France that effaced from the pediments of its buildings the motto Liberty, Equality, Fraternity—triumphed under the banner of Vichy. But this second France, tainted by its collaboration with the occupying Nazi forces, collapsed in the face of the Liberation. For a while it seemed as if the democratic, socially responsible France had established itself once and for all. In recent years, however, we have witnessed the resurgence of a rampant Vichyism that cannot be attributed to any military disaster, campaign of collaboration, or occupying forces. We do not have space to analyze the national and more generalized factors that have driven this plunge into the past. Let us just say that the dissolution of a strong belief in historical progress, the growing uncertainties of the present, waves of economic turbulence, and the crisis of civilization at large taken together are a source of anxiety and anguish that, in the absence of hope for a better future, drive many to take refuge in the certainties of the past, to retreat to a twisted conception of national identity, to make foreigners and immigrants scapegoats, viewing them as enemies who have infiltrated their own country.

A closed culture that has lost its inherent vitality can tolerate no more than a trickle of immigration. Such a culture is incapable of incorporating new arrivals into its social fabric. An open, living culture, in contrast, can take in immigrants in great numbers.

The converging and worsening crises of civilization, society, and the economy combine to aggravate the danger. The cracks in society become fissures and crevices, the marginalized and the excluded grow in number, and we wander like so many sleepwalkers toward disasters that we can sense looming but that remain cloaked in the mists of the future. The stock market crash of 1929 triggered the legal rise to power of the Nazis in an anguished, frustrated, jangled society; that rise in turn began a process of spreading conflict that led to the Second World War. The current crisis is exacerbating all existing ruptures, fears, and hatreds, and is plunging us into new abysses. The crisis of the democracies is exacerbated by the economic slowdown, and these converging crises encourage the rise of extremists. The resulting picture is inadequately defined by the word "populism," even less so given the fact that the left, itself in a state of crisis, has not yet succeeded in directing the growing sense of discontent toward any liberating outcome, and the populist forces, which have been so active in the past, are now fragmented or off-kilter. Moreover, the generalized feelings of powerlessness and resignation threaten in short order to turn into blind rage and frenzy. Hence the urgent need for a new form of thought and a new political approach in all domains.

The Politics of Quality of Life

All the major and minor ills that we have pointed out, factors in political, social, and cultural decline, are in turn sources of an array of multiple deteriorations of the quality of our everyday lives. To fight those ills, we must implement in-depth reforms of both the society we live in and the way we live. We need to overturn and invert the dictatorship of quantity over quality while continuing to supply the amount of goods and services needed to prevent need and destitution.

It is essential that we ensure growth and the fulfillment of independence, while integrating those factors into larger communities, and revive a sense of fellowship and discourage selfishness. It is our right to do more than merely survive (that is, more than simply meet our obligations without joy or happiness). And it is our responsibility to see life as part and parcel of growth and fulfillment in relation to other people and with the world. Excitement and wonder and aesthetic pleasure are more than a set of luxuries reserved for the elite; everyone deserves them.

With this end in mind, we propose a path that entails at once a new economic and social policy, a labor policy that both reduces bureaucracy and lessens emphasis on "competitivity," a new urban strategy and a shift in priorities toward the countryside, new programs concerning agricultural production, a new attitude toward consumption—all of which are diverse and complementary components of an overall policy of quality of life.

Quality of life may at first sound like a synonym for welfare and well-being. But the very notion of well-being has dwindled in contemporary civilization to the strictly material sense that implies comfort, wealth and ownership. These have nothing to do with what really constitutes well-being: furthering personal growth and fulfillment, relationships of friendship and love, and a sense of community. Well-being and quality of life nowadays must certainly include material well-being, but not a merely quantitative conception that chases after always getting more. It means quality of life, not quantity of possessions. It entails, first and foremost, emotional, psychic, and moral well-being.

In opposition to the dictatorship of quantity, calculation, and ownership, we must encourage a broader policy of quality of life, that is to say, once again, of living well (what the sociologist Alain Caillé calls a "politics of conviviality"). With that objective in mind, we must discourage the multiple factors that undermine the quality of air, food, water, health, and climate. Any gain in energy efficiency necessarily translates to an improvement in health and quality of life.

Detoxifying city centers plagued by an addiction to automobiles will reduce the incidence of respiratory diseases and psychosomatic afflictions. Reducing our dependence upon industrial farming and livestock breeding will necessarily benefit rural farmers, and cleaning up and reclaiming our water tables—our source for clean, safe water—will help to restore the quality of our food supply and safeguard consumer safety and health. Weaning ourselves off our addiction to superfluous goods that pretend to offer seduction and enjoyment, our squandering of disposable objects, and the rapid succession of fashions that make products obsolete in the blink of an eye will allow us to reverse course and halt the frenzied race after the "new and improved" in favor of a calm pursuit of "truly good and better." That pursuit will take place within a continuous process favoring two essential currents: the rehumanization of our cities and the revitalization of our countryside. Both of those processes are necessary if we are to maintain the quality of our lives. The latter process entails reviving small towns and villages by the introduction of telecommuting; the return of the local baker, the bistro, the post office, the elementary school; the maintenance of the local roads and public transportation. Revitalization and repopulation of the countryside go hand in hand.

At the same time, we must reform public administrations and corporate administration. In this context, we must debureaucratize, derigidify, and decompartmentalize. We must offer initiatives and opportunities to civil servants and corporate employees to become more agile. We have to make sure that kindness, patience, and attention are given to all those who interact with public offices, beginning with the elderly and those who face challenges with language or lack a solid command of mathematics. The reform of the state does not depend on increasing or decreasing the number of jobs, but rather results from no longer considering human beings as objects that can be quantified but as living beings endowed with autonomy, intelligence, and emotions.

Well-being entails individual growth and fulfillment within the context of a community of relations. Our lives are polarized between the prose of everyday life, a life that we experience out of obligation or duty, and the poetic aspect, which brings fullness, fervor, and exaltation to our lives. This is the experience that we find in love, friendship, collective activities, celebrations, dances, and amusements. The prose of everyday life is necessary to our survival. But poetry is necessary for us truly to live. Our politics of a successful or vibrant civilization allows our fellow men and women to fully express their poetic inner lives.

The Revitalization of Fellowship

If we wish to create a society that enjoys true quality of life, we must revitalize the fellowship that is a crucial element of solidarity. We propose creating a network of community centers in medium-sized and large cities, as well as in neighborhoods and quarters of a metropolis the size of New York. This network of community centers would bring together under a single roof all the public and private social services and institutions that now exist, as well as offer a new array of services that provide urgent aid to the victims of moral or physical abuse. They would come to the rescue of the victims of overdoses—not only drug overdoses but also overdoses of malaise and grief. In light of the barriers to admittance to modern hospitals, these centers would constitute dispensaries providing urgent care for a variety of ills.

When the structures of society were authoritarian, family based, and far more rigid, individuals were psychically straitjacketed within an array of strictures and norms, resulting in countless frustrations and limitations. The growth of individual independence within the family and society at large has contributed, in the context of a lack of strong and durable community ties, to the proliferation of breakups and divorces. These are powerful factors leading to multiple neuroses, misery, loneliness, and psychic disturbances that demand love and attention, the little bit of care that brings comfort and relief.

Likewise, the community centers will be sources of friendship and care for others. They will serve a diverse and articulated mission as venues for social initiatives, interpersonal mediations, empathy, compassion, assistance, information, volunteerism, and activism.

At the same time, it has become urgent that we establish a civic service of brotherhood and sisterhood. This institution would not only come to the service of the community centers but also would offer assistance in case of collective disasters—floods, earthquakes, heat waves, droughts, and so on. They would operate on every continent as well; generosity, empathy, and altruism will become intrinsic to the reformed society to which we aspire.

The revitalization of fellowship is part and parcel of certain reforms. Among them are the debureaucratizing of civil servants and white-collar corporate workers, restoring to them that dimension of free will and personal initiative they long ago lost by behaving like robots. This would allow them to communicate with one another as well as with the consumers who use their services. As a result, they will gain a conscience and awareness of what fellowship means in the workplace. The reform of education will open young minds to the fundamental and global challenges of their futures as individuals and as citizens, and the indissoluble link of individuals to their social milieu.

In our conception of brotherhood, juvenile delinquents are still at a malleable age. It is our responsibility to ensure that they have every opportunity for rehabilitation and redemption. We should especially look upon immigrants as our brothers who have emerged from poverty and deprivation, not as interlopers to be kept at arm's length. After all, the poverty from which they are escaping was in many instances created by our colonization of their homelands in the past, or even engendered by the introduction of our economic system in their countries. Colonization and the imposition of Western economic systems frequently result in the destruction of subsistence-based polycultures. They lead to the migration of rural, agrarian populations into the misery of urban shantytowns and favelas. They ensure that grim corruption reigns over the highest offices of state.

Let us not minimize issues of crime and public safety, especially those that affect people who travel through or live in certain outlying areas of the major cities. As we are taught by the situation in the United States, however, police repression does little more than encourage the growth and spread of crime and delinquency; prisons serve as authentic incubators for these larger phenomena. We must grasp once and for all the idea that those whom our society rejects will only reject that society in return and reject us along with it. We therefore call for a policy of crime prevention that rejects the very idea of that rejection. We cannot limit our intervention to measures designed to expand residential settlement, which goes hand in hand with gentrification, or surveillance cameras, or the establishment of satellite police stations in high-crime areas. We must not settle for a new form of urban planning and a revision of our management of territorial administration. We must also implement a caring policy of humanization. From local examples to Medellín in Colombia, to Rio de Janeiro with its complex of favelas, to Caracas, where a symphony orchestra was created with young people from the shantytowns—all provide one clear lesson: If we recognize the personal dignity and worth of children and young people, if we give them access to education, computer technology, and the arts, and most important of all, if we offer them understanding and love, juvenile delinquency will diminish drastically.

Youth Policies

We must set forth a youth policy that recognizes what an adolescent is in sociological and cultural terms. Adolescents are the weakest links in society's chain (because they are the least integrated into society's fabric, caught between the cocoon of childhood and full membership in the ranks of adulthood) and at the same time the strongest links in that chain (because they are endowed with the greatest amount of energy, the most vigorous ambitions, the greatest capacity for revolt and rebellion). Youth can be an explosive and liberating force, but also an unbridled and destructive power when it is marginalized and ghettoized. We saw clear cases of this truth in the Paris region in 2005, and again in London in the summer of 2011. A youth policy not only engenders solidarity and fellowship through civil service. It also guides us to a fellow feeling for the problems of youth as well as recognition of the inherent *dignity* of all the young people that society has rejected.

Remoralization

Because ethics is drawn from personal responsibility and social solidarity, everything that we have set forth above contributes to the ethical revitalization and, more broadly, the general remoralization of a society that is currently being degraded and undermined by spreading irresponsibility and the expansion and amplification of corruption.

Corruption has become a major issue. It is a problem that plagues public administrations, the state, and candidates who win elections. Corruption has spread to all walks of life because of the reigning values of money and the deterioration of standards that tend to restrict selfishness and egotism. No process of remoralization can be satisfied with mere lessons in morality. It must begin by challenging the uncontrasted reign of the profit motive and by illuminating the importance of solidarity and fellowship. At the same time, it is necessary to restore standards of morality for public servants and officials—first of all by example, and over time by increasingly stringent enforcement. The same applies to all professions that involve a mission and a fiduciary responsibility toward society (physicians, teachers, judges, elected officials, and so on). That is why we advocate the creation of a state council for ethics (formed of elected officials, members of the judiciary and law enforcement, educators, well-known figures in the arts and humanities, humanitarian activists, and so on) that can plan and implement a campaign to teach values of Confucian benevolence and responsibility to all those who wish to undertake a public career that entails responsibility or power or both.

Labor and Employment

The crisis in the world of work is twofold, affecting working conditions and employment.

Working conditions have become increasingly unpleasant and hostile. One main factor is the speedup imposed on workers by the pressures of cutthroat competition and the growing demands of productivity (taking the metrics we use for machinery and equipment and applying them to human beings). The reform that we have sketched out entails introducing into business and public administration an authentically human form of rational productivity. Such an approach would restore communications between compartmentalized sectors and encourage both creative initiatives and the involvement of one and all in the resulting whole. Scheduling should be based on the degree of interest of the work, the fatigue factor, and safety, rather than by dictating a fixed number of hours (the forty-hour workweek, for instance). Likewise, we propose modifying some retirement ages and eliminating a prescribed retirement age in those professions where age is irrelevant. This is already the case in politics, the arts, research, university teaching, and so on. Of course this requires regular checkups to monitor workers' mental and physical health. Otherwise, depending on the nature of the work and the interests of the workers, retirement age would not be mandated.

In terms of employment, we propose stimulating the creation and development of all activities that contribute to the quality of life. The welfare state is in decline everywhere even though the basic achievements that it brought about still remain intact (though for how much longer?). A new kind of social assistance is necessary. Not only must we provide aid to the sick, the unemployed, and the poverty-stricken; public assistance must also extend to the creation of businesses and services necessary to the collective quality of life. Thus, the social-investment state must complement the existence of the welfare state.

The Economic Multi-reform: The Pluralistic Economy

We advocate a fair and equitable economy, both socially responsible and characterized by solidarity in the context of a larger and pluralistic economy.

Those who denounce capitalism are incapable of theorizing an even minimally credible alternative; those who consider capitalism immortal are resigned to it. Social democracy has fallen silent on the subject of what was once its principal enemy.

Instead of resignation in the face of a capitalism that is considered immortal, or the contrary belief that capitalism is in its death throes, a pluralistic economy incorporates the capitalist economy and the various multinational companies, but it progressively restricts its sphere of operation. The pluralistic economy abolishes its all-powerful status, while taking great care to exercise strict control over finance capitalism.

A pluralistic economy works to develop small and medium-sized businesses, and encourages the economics of social solidarity, fair trade, and ethical business practices.

1. *A socially responsible form of economics that promotes fellowship* entails encouraging cooperatives of production and consumption, professional organizations and solidarity associations, ethical savings and loans and institutes of microcredit, and establishing new legislative and fiscal measures designed to finance local projects that create jobs.

2. *An economy predicated on fairness* leads to the deployment of a form of fair trade that safeguards the interests of small producers and manufacturers, on the one hand, by restricting

and eliminating predatory middlemen and, on the other hand, by maintaining a price level that is adequate to buffer the market against fluctuations in the availability and price of raw materials. It requires neutralizing predatory practices by large-scale middlemen, especially in terms of the consumption of foods, where producers are forced to accept too low a price and consumers are forced to pay too high a price.

3. *A green economy* entails not only replacing pollution-producing forms of energy with healthier forms, and therefore installing new means of production of green energy (solar power, wind power, hydraulic power, geothermal power). It also involves large-scale projects for urban humanization and depollution. It will lead to a reduction of government subsidies for industrialized agriculture and redistribute those same subventions to farm-based or organic agriculture.

We must undertake a modern version of the New Deal by launching large-scale infrastructure projects. These projects create jobs, drastically lower unemployment, and improve the economy. In contrast, the policy of budget cutting leads only to a worsening of the recession, more job losses, a drop in salaries and revenues, and a reduction in consumption. That, in turn, worsens the social crisis while claiming to improve the economic crisis.

Encouraging local food consumption would provide us with farm-raised high-quality products and prepare us to better withstand the food crises that are increasingly likely to sweep the planet.

4. *All politics must take into account environmental and ecological issues* among the fundamental concerns bound up with quality of life, but it cannot be restricted to ecology. The progressive retreat from the realm of nuclear fission must go hand in hand with continuing research into nuclear fusion. In order to better inform the citizenry concerning these issues, we propose the creation of a panel of investigation into the overdevelopment of nuclear power, the shortage of reliable information about risks, and the underdevelopment of renewable power.

5. *The state as an investor in society.* The welfare state is increasingly being ravaged by globalization. We need to safeguard the basic guarantees that it has maintained or created. At the same time, it's necessary to develop the state as a large-scale social investor. Social investment by the state includes encouraging with credits (which can be repaid, in case of success) all the creations of small- and medium-scale businesses in the areas of health, community interaction, various forms of aid, and the aesthetics of everyday life. The state as investor must commit to a new New Deal by undertaking a policy of major public works in order to develop piggyback railroad facilities, widen and dredge canals, create belts of parking facilities around cities and downtown areas, encourage consumers to use nonpolluting public transportation and individual means of transport. All this will make it possible to create jobs and at the same time enhance the quality of life. The expense of major public works to increase healthful lifestyles in major cities will be more than paid for over the years by the decrease in

sociopsychosomatic illnesses caused by stress, pollution, and poor health.

6. *Free and fair competition* can thrive only in a marketplace that is governed by rules. Cutthroat competition is an exaggerated version of free and fair competition that undermines working conditions and leads to firings. Those firings, in turn, increase the burden of work placed on those who still have their jobs. Because cutthroat competition is "justified" by the need to respond to the low costs of imported goods, we propose taxing imported goods whose low price is due to the extreme exploitation of workers who are not free, as in China. Whenever the lower prices are due to the exploitation of workers who are paid below-subsistence-level wages, are forbidden to organize into unions, and who do not enjoy a pluralistic political system, a tariff should be leveled on those imports. This is a clear illustration of our twofold imperative: globalize and deglobalize, with the latter resulting in variable and temporary customs tariffs in order to protect from utter destruction certain local, regional, or national economies.

7. *We will restrict financial speculation* by closely monitoring and controlling the banks, vigilantly supervising the credit-rating agencies, taxing short-term transactions, prohibiting speculation on price fluctuations, enacting an antitrust law against monopolies and oligopolies, and acting internationally to eliminate tax havens.

8. *Develop subsidies for farm-based and organic agriculture* rather than for industrialized agriculture and livestock breeding.

9. *A payment for underprivileged families*, modeled on the Brazilian Bolsa Família, will enable them to pay for the education of their children and their most urgent needs.

All of these measures will restrict the domain of capitalism, the dictatorship of the profit motive, and the power of financial lobbies within our democratic system. They will bring about a genuine revival of the economy by directly fostering preferred sectors, especially the green economy, and by discouraging the worst aspects—the economics of waste, the superfluous, the disposable, as well as products with mythological or illusory value. This will lead to an enhanced quality of life.

Consumer Policies

The new economic policies will coexist with a new politics of consumption.

Underconsumption is prevalent among the poorer classes, who should be supplied more than just unleavened bread, hormone-injected poultry, meat from artificially fattened livestock, and preserved foods with potentially harmful ingredients. A nutritional charter that called for reductions in price (with the difference reimbursed by the national or regional governments, much like discounted meal tickets) would allow the underprivileged to eat fresh, tasty, and healthful foods.

On the other hand, among the middle class and the poorer classes, there is overconsumption of all sorts of unhealthful products loaded with salt or sugar. The sugary foods marketed today are factors in the epidemic of child and adolescent obesity; the young are conditioned by advertising to consume sweets until they are victims of genuine sugar addictions. There is overconsumption of products whose beneficial qualities are either exaggerated or illusory, products that promise health, beauty, longevity, rejuvenation, and virility. Consumers have only the narrowest margins of conscious choice. Few publications provide reliable information about the actual value of foods or other products. With little awareness of what is healthful and what is not, consumers are frequently seduced by advertisements to buy less healthful—and more expensive—foods.

Individual, scattered consumers are powerless. But joined together, they constitute a considerable civic force that wields the power of selective purchasing and boycott, which can in turn affect the quality and the price of products. At the same time, it can encourage the quality of life.

We propose that a public consumer agency be created to educate consumers (and introduce consumption as a subject to be taught in secondary schools nationwide). This agency would monitor the quality of products and the honesty of advertising. It would encourage the coordination of existing associations in a national league of consumers.

It would support the growth of farming in the areas around major cities, to guarantee the availability of locally sourced food products. This would help to discourage the consumption of expensive imported summer crops in winter. It would help to protect local breeders of sheep, pigs, and cattle by levying a special tax on the mass breeding of livestock on distant continents. We would also reinforce the means available for tracing imported foods.

Inequalities

The increase in inequality resulting from the omnipotence of free-market capitalism has resulted in a proliferation of all forms of poverty. It has also accentuated the slide from poor to poverty-stricken, as well as intensified the levels of corruption within the governing class, while a minuscule oligarchy takes full advantage of out-rageous tax privileges.

Over the short term, we propose the establish-ment of three permanent councils.

1. *A permanent council to fight inequality*, which would begin by attacking levels of excess (of bene-fits and salaries at the very top) and inadequacy (of quality and prosperity of life at the bottom). Its mission would be to oversee the annual increase of the lowest revenues and the reduction of the highest revenues. Against the uncertainties and crippling effects of poverty, the council would es-tablish a tax safety net to protect the deprived and the underprivileged, as well as an intensive policy of homebuilding.

2. *A permanent council in charge of reversing the imbalance* in labor-capital relations that has steadily grown since 1990.

3. *A permanent council in charge of the social and human transformations* that are needed in order to counter the natural, biological, and social prob-lems engendered by damage to Earth's biosphere:

the battle against urban and rural industrial pollution, the development of renewable energy, the protection and improvement of the quality of life.

A solemn appeal on the part of the citizenry will be addressed to the superwealthy in order to persuade them to envision for themselves a latter-day Night of August 4th,* an occasion on which they would officially renounce a part of their wealth, as certain American billionaires, like Warren Buffett, have already done, either by giving away a portion of their fortune or else demanding an increase in the taxes they pay. This is in any case an excellent opportunity to review from top to bottom the basis of our tax structure and to revise our overall fiscal approach.

Education

We must institute vast reforms in order to attain a more democratic educational system.

---

* On August 4, 1789, the French Estates-General gave up their privileges and formally abolished feudalism.

We should restore the dignity of the teaching profession, and put a halt to the relentless drive to eliminate teaching positions. We also need to undertake a deep-seated reform on the basis of the principle set forth by Rousseau in the *Emile*: "Life is the trade I want to teach him." This means providing each student with the resources to allow him or her to face and resolve the fundamental and global problems that challenge every individual, all societies, and humanity as a whole. These problems are far too often fragmented by the specialization of compartmentalized disciplines.

No improvement in the sector of elementary education, so crucial to the entire edifice of the national educational system, can take place without a complete revision of the basic approach to teacher training. One vital factor is fostering a system of education that can effectively promote the brightest of the underprivileged students. Another crucial factor is that we value the profession (too often considered nothing more than a second family income), as well as direct the most experienced and enthusiastic teachers toward the most challenging classes and areas.

The basic purpose of higher education is to enable the younger generations to grapple with the crucial problems affecting their lives as individuals, citizens, and people of Planet Earth, during the formative and decisive years of adolescence. In that context, education must take on the fundamental global problems of our lives and of our time, which in turn demands the cooperation of scientific and academic disciplines that have long remained walled off one from another.

It is of the utmost importance not only to provide knowledge but also to infuse an understanding of what knowledge really *is*, threatened as it is by dogmatism, wrongheadedness, illusions, and simplemindedness. This means furnishing students with a useful body of knowledge.

Our schools must teach not merely humanism but also what a human being really *is*, in our threefold nature as biological, individual, and social entities. This will produce a clear understanding of the human condition, its history, its complexity, its contradictions, its successes, and its tragedies.

Students must acquire a human appreciation that allows us to establish fellowship and brotherhood, to grasp both our own identity and our differences from others, and to acknowledge the complexity of that identity and those differences, rather than reducing them to a single and negative caricature.

Equally important is an understanding of the global era that humanity is now experiencing, the opportunities that it offers and the risks that it poses, including all the most vital problems—for each of us and for all of us.

It is critical that we face up to the uncertainties that each individual inevitably encounters in his or her own life, in the larger life of the collective, and in the history of nations, uncertainties that have been greatly exacerbated at this dawn of the twenty-first century: for ourselves as individuals, for our societies, and for all of humanity.

It is likewise urgent that our educational system focus on the problems of modern civilization that affect our everyday lives: issues of family life, youth culture, urban problems, the relations between city and countryside (the problems of humanizing the cities and revitalizing the countryside), consumption, leisure time, mass media, and the active pursuit and exercise of democratic liberties . . .

The university, in turn, takes on a twofold mission: The first task is to adapt to the modern world in social terms and in terms of scientific research and academic scholarship, to integrate and provide professional education; the second task is to create a metaprofessional culture, transsecular in nature, encompassing the autonomy of consciousness, problem solving, the primacy of truth over utility, and the ethics of knowledge. That culture, which transcends the fleeting forms of the here and now, can nevertheless help the citizenry to attain their goals in the here and now.

These two missions work together and clash at the same time—to adapt to society and to shape society so that it adapts to us. One links to the other in a loop that can prove fertile. It is not merely a question of modernizing culture; it is also important to establish a culture of modernity.

Many obstacles in the present-day environment challenge that twofold mission. First, a habitual pressure on education and research to adapt to the economic, technical, and administrative demands of the present, to subscribe to the latest methods and the most recent recipes on the market—which means reducing liberal arts education and marginalizing humanistic culture. Throughout history, extreme adaptation to existing conditions has been less a sign of vitality than an indicator of decline and death through a loss of imagination and creativity.

Moreover, compartmentalization and an array of barriers exist between humanistic culture and scientific culture, barriers that go hand in hand with the compartmentalization between various sciences and other disciplines. The lack of communication between the two cultures risks grave consequences for both. The humanistic culture revitalizes the works of the past; the scientific culture focuses on the discoveries of the present. Humanism is a general culture that, through philosophy, essays, and novels, poses fundamental human problems and encourages reflection. Scientific culture encourages a form of thought devoted to theory, not a reflection on man's fate or the future of science itself. Scientific culture provides fundamental knowledge and understanding concerning the universe, life, and human beings, but it is devoid of a reflexive and introspective dimension. The mill of humanistic culture no longer receives and grinds the crucial wheat of scientific knowledge. The boundary between the two cultures runs straight through the heart of sociology and, as a result, that discipline finds itself split in two rather than providing a shuttle that links the two.

All this demands a reform of the way we think. Medieval knowledge was far too strictly organized and therefore easily took the form of a tidy and consistent summa. Contemporary knowledge is fragmented, dispersive, and compartmentalized. A reorganization of knowledge is already under way. Environmental science, earth sciences, and cosmology are all multidisciplinary disciplines that treat not a limited sector cut free of all context but a complex system: the ecosystem—or, more broadly, the biosphere—for environmental science; the earth as a system for earth sciences; and the strange propensity of the universe for forming and destroying the systems that comprise galaxies and solar systems, for cosmology.

Everywhere we see a growing recognition of the need for an interdisciplinary approach and a looming awareness of the need for a trans-disciplinary approach—to the study of health, aging, architecture and urban studies, energy, synthetic materials, and artworks produced by new technologies.

But a transdisciplinary approach to art and science is only one solution in the context of a larger and more complex school of thought. We must replace our way of thinking that breaks things down with a mind-set that knits things to-gether, and that linkage demands that a unilin-ear and unidirectional concept of causation be replaced by a looped, multireferential concept of causation, that the rigidity of classical logic be corrected by a dialectic capable of entertaining notions that are at the same time complementary and antagonistic, and that an understanding of the integration of elements into a whole necessitates an appreciation of the integration of everything within those elements.

Another goal is to reform our way of thinking in order to put an end to the decline of democracy that has led, in all fields of politics, to the rise of the unquestioned authority of experts and specialists in all fields. This has correspondingly undermined the authority of citizens. We blindly accept decisions issued by those who are supposed to know, but who, in actual practice, possess only a fragmentary and abstract knowledge, a narrow understanding that ignores the crucial global and contextual nature of problems. The development of a cognitive democracy is possible only within the larger context of a reorganization of knowledge. In order to achieve that, we must call for a reform of the way we think. Then we will find ourselves doing more than separating analytically in order to understand; we will also begin knitting together that which has been analytically sundered.

We are talking about a reform that is much broader and deeper, a reform without which a democratization of university-level education remains incapable of having any decisive effect on the awareness and consciousness of our young people. This is not therefore a programmatic reform; it is a paradigmatic reform, which involves our very ability to organize our knowledge and understanding.

At the same time, and by the same token, we will succeed in regenerating our larger general culture, because all of us, in order to understand our essential humanity, need to be able to understand our own place in the world, our lives, our society, our history.

The Culture of Aesthetics

A considerable portion of culture is aesthetic in nature—literature, music, painting. We believe that any politics based on the quality of life must foster the poetic aspects of life, which entail the capacity for emotional involvement, admiration, and a sense of wonder. Encouraging aesthetic culture will help us all to live in a more poetic fashion. Often, in the midst of aesthetic involvement, we find that we are more deeply human; at the movies, for instance, we are able to understand and love those whom we normally ignore and mistrust in everyday life—the homeless, the criminals, the enemy—because we are made aware, on the screen, of human aspects of their personality that we otherwise tend to reject as inhuman.

The world is wonderful and horrible.

Aesthetics helps us to appreciate wonder and at the same time to look horror in the face. Thus, many of the great symphonies express the worst grief and pain of the soul while also offering us an ineffable musical joy.

The aesthetics of art and literature and music will help us to develop an aesthetics of everyday life. Nature imitates what art suggests, it has been said.

This is what should drive all cultural policies: a politics of aesthetics that helps to spread and democratize the poetry of life and living, that ensures that everyone can experience positive beautiful feelings, that we are one and all allowed to discover our own personal truths through the masterpieces of art, just as the two authors of this book have been privileged to do.

The State

The state has been greatly weakened by the effects of a globalized economy, by a growing and increasingly radical integration into the European Union, and by the loss of entire sectors of public service to privatization. Moreover, in the last few decades, a fair number of powers have been delegated from the central government to regional governments.

While still pursuing the goal of European integration, in particular in areas that have thus far been rejected by our more liberal partners, and while continuing to pursue the positive aspects of globalization, we propose preserving government subsidies as an oppositional complement to globalization.

The Reform of Politics and the Revitalization of Democracy

There is no question that we are experiencing a degeneration, a withering of democracy. The drift into oligarchy is only one of those processes. The loss of political vigor among the citizenry is at the root of the drift, as is the lack of a cognitive democracy—the inability of the citizens to attain sufficient technical and scientific knowledge to allow them to understand and to treat an increasingly complex array of problems.

There are great and urgent material, economic, and technological needs, and we should surely work to satisfy them. There are, however, other necessities—to start with, the need to be acknowledged as a human being in full—that drive those whom the interests of profiteering and cutthroat competition have reduced to objects considered purely in terms of financial calculation, the people in society who have been ignored, forgotten, mistreated, humiliated, held in contempt, and "dumpsterized." The politics of the quality of life is designed to combat not only physical and material poverty but also moral distress, loneliness, humiliations, contempt, deprivation, and misunderstandings (through directed education, beginning in elementary schools, to an understanding of our fellow man).

The reform of political thought will ultimately result in our ability to consider and effectively respond to the challenge of fundamental and global problems that are inseparable from the reforms that we propose: the humanization and the rehumanization of society. *These reforms will themselves be the product of and the driving force behind the politics of the quality of life. This new political approach will open a prospect for the future, a fountain of hope, and it will bind the nation together in a wave of fellowship that will spring from that fountain of hope.*

The driving force behind this great reform will emerge once it becomes clear that it is a response to that nation's needs and aspirations. That weighed down by a creaking and increasingly arteriosclerotic burden of bureaucratic structures, our country—all countries—are bursting with life deep within. A clear demonstration of that fact was the remarkable response to the appeal in *Time for Outrage*, a response that was not limited to France but spread throughout the world, taken as an invitation to risk the discussion of unacceptably grim consequences.[3] Individual change and social change are inseparable; taken alone, each is inadequate. The reform of politics, the reform of thought, the reform of society, the reform of the way we live—all of these will converge to produce a larger metamorphosis of society. The radiant futures of the past are now dead, but we will show the way to a possible glowing future.

The path toward a politics based on the quality of life cannot be undertaken and developed unless we make up our minds to throttle the octopus of finance capitalism and the barbarity of national purification and ethnic cleansing. Finance capitalism is not the same as productive capitalism; in fact, it feeds parasitically off productive capitalism and diverts capital from the sectors of production and manufacturing into profit taking and speculation. But productive capitalism is currently being twisted by productivity and cutthroat competition—forces that are working, as we have said, to the detriment of laborers who are subjected to miserable conditions and the threat of losing their jobs. Productive capitalism has several aspects: reasonable and temporary tariffs and trade barriers, the revival of labor organizing, and a broader regeneration of the left to rein in the worst excesses of capitalist exploitation, just as was the case in the past for the Western nations. Thus, the combined reforms that we are proposing will drive back in all sectors the dictatorship of the profit motive and result in the abolition of financial speculation.

The forces of barbarity and national purification led to the Spanish Inquisition and the expulsion of Muslims and Jews from Spain in 1492. They caused the wars of religion of the sixteenth and seventeenth centuries throughout Europe, and resulted in the ethnic cleansing and Nazi genocide of the twentieth century.

Once again this force threatens European nations, as well as the rest of the world. It fosters forms of fanaticism that strive to purify and expel, rooted conceptually, like all forms of fanaticism, in two distinct notions: on the one hand, Manichaeism, which satanizes all those whom one wishes to reject or destroy, and on the other hand, the reducing of the other to the worst aspects (both real and imaginary) of their persona. The struggle against extremism and Manichaeism cannot restrict itself to an appeal to rational thought; it can become effective only if alongside it we develop, through a vigorous reform of the educational system, a complex way of thought that is capable of seeing as a single whole various diverse or ambivalent characteristics of a single phenomenon, a single population, or a single person, including oneself.

We must therefore fight this battle on two fronts, not against a single enemy; this twofold struggle will clear the way for a politics of the quality of life.

People are rising up more or less everywhere on Earth, in spite of their extreme diversity, in opposition to the worst aspects of the unbridled power of money: in the Arab nations, Israel, India, Chile, Spain, Greece, Iceland . . . Almost everywhere in the world, it is goodwill that has led these revolts. But these insurrections lack a body of political thought to underpin their efforts to organize and guide these forces.

We can blaze this path toward a new way of politics here in France; we can work to spread it and assure its acceptance throughout Europe and the rest of the world. We want to show the way to planetary salvation.

Regeneration

We are not trying to found a new party, nor are we rallying adherence to an existing party. We are calling for a political rebirth by drawing on three sources of inspiration that have traditionally fed the political left: libertarianism, which focuses on the liberty of individuals; socialism, which concentrates on the bettering of society; communism, which emphasizes the brotherhood of a community. Let us add a fourth: environmentalism, which restores our ties to and our interdependence with nature and, on a deeper level, with Mother Earth, as well as recognizes in our sun the source of all living energy.

We call for all existing political parties, whose sources of inspiration and direction have long since dried up and in many cases become fossilized, to agree to be broken up in order to allow the foundation of a new political structure that would draw simultaneously on all four political sources.

We are not calling for a pact among existing political parties. We urge them to aid in the creation of a powerful citizen movement, a broad insurrection of conscience that alone can engender a form of politics that is equal to the challenges that now face it.

We have done our best here to define it.[4] We feel certain that if it leads and sets an example, it can spread throughout Europe and from there to the rest of the planet, thus helping a politics of humanity to thrive and grow.

Our proposals are not meant to be exhaustive; they are set forth in order to be critiqued, completed, and reshaped. But there is one thing that we feel sure of: Today we are sorely in need of a new form of politics, a politics based on a yearning to live and restore life, a politics that uproots us from our present-day apathy and mortal resignation. This politics of a yearning for life takes on the features of a politics of the quality of life much as we have outlined them here.

The yearning for life will feed the quality of life, and the quality of life will foster a yearning for life. Together, they will both blaze a path to hope.

Notes

1. "Discours sur l'histoire," *Variété* 4, 1932.

2. Konrad Lorenz, *Civilized Man's Eight Deadly Sins* (New York: Harcourt, 1974), p. 27.

3. *Time for Outrage* (New York: Twelve, 2011).

4. We are not alone in leading the way for this new political approach. Let us mention a few names: Patrick Viveret, director of the Dialogues en Humanité conferences; Claude Alphandéry, a pioneer of a socially responsible form of economics that involves solidarity; Alain Caillé, *De la convivialité*; Hervé Sérieyx and André-Yves Portnoff, *Aux actes citoyens!*; Camille Landais, Thomas Piketty, and Emmanuel Saez, *Pour une revolution fiscal*; Pierre Larrouturou, *Pour éviter le krach ultime*; and the "Économistes Atterrés," or Appalled Economists. All these lines of thought, all these bodies of work, are now converging and cross-pollinating.

A writer and a poet, a hero of the French Resistance, and one of the drafters of the United Nations' Universal Declaration of Human Rights, **STÉPHANE HESSEL** was on *Foreign Policy* magazine's list of the top global thinkers of 2011. His short book *Time for Outrage!* has sold four million copies in thirty languages since it was released in October 2010.

Ninety-year-old **EDGAR MORIN** is also a former member of the French Resistance who has continued his fight against barbarity in every shape and form. A prominent scholar, widely recognized as one of the most important French thinkers of our time, he has authored books on sociology and philosophy that have been translated in forty-two countries.

JEFF MADRICK is an author, a regular contributor to *The New York Review of Books*, and a former economics columnist for *The New York Times*. He is editor of *Challenge Magazine* and a senior fellow and Director of the Rediscovering Government Project at the Roosevelt Institute. He is also a senior fellow at the Schwartz Center for Economic Policy Analysis, The New School. He has written for many of the nation's most prominent publications, and has appeared on all the major television and cable networks, as well as public television and public radio. He has written a half-dozen acclaimed books. His most recent is *Age of Greed: The Rise of Finance and the Decline of America, 1970 to the Present.*

ANTONY SHUGAAR's recent translations include books by Simonetta Agnello Hornby, Silvia Avallone, Nanni Balestrini (with an NEA fellowship), Massimo Carlotto, Diego De Silva, Giorgio Faletti, Gianni Rodari, and Paolo Sorrentino. He is the author of *Coast to Coast* and *I Lie for a Living* and the coauthor, with the late Gianni Guadalupi, of *Discovering America* and *Latitude Zero.*

Notes

Notes

Notes

Notes

Notes

Notes

Notes

Notes

Notes